Sweet Land of Liberty

CAROL J. ENDRES

HARVEST HOUSE™ PUBLISHERS

EUGENE, OREGON

Sweet Land of Liberty

Copyright © 2002 by Carol Endres
Published by Harvest House Publishers
Eugene, OR 97402

Artwork designs are copyrighted by Carol Endres and reproduced under license from Endres Studios, Kinderhook, NY and may not be reproduced without permission. For information regarding art prints featured in this book, please contact:

Endres Studios
P.O. Box 640
Kinderhook, NY 12106
(518) 758-2170

Library of Congress Cataloging-in-Publication Data

Endres, Carol, 1948-
   Sweet land of liberty / Carol Endres.
      p. cm.
   ISBN 0-7369-0749-1 (hardback : alk. paper)
  1. Endres, Carol, 1948–Catalogs. 2. Primitivism in art–United States–Catalogs. 3. Patriotism in art–Catalogs. I. Title.
   ND237.E617 A4 2002a
   709' .2–dc21

2002002161

Design and Production by Garborg Design Works, Minneapolis, Minnesota

Harvest House Publishers has made every effort to trace the ownership of all poems and quotes. In the event of a question arising from the use of a poem or quote, we regret any error made and will be pleased to make the necessary correction in future editions of this book.

Unless otherwise indicated, Scriptures are taken from the Holy Bible: New International Version ®. NIV ®. Copyright © 1973, 1978, 1984 by the International Bible Society. Used by permission of Zondervan Publishing House. Scriptures marked KJV are from the King James Version.

Printed in China.

02 03 04 05 06 07 08 09 10 11 / RP / 10 9 8 7 6 5 4 3 2 1

AMERICA, GOD'S RESOLVE

God's resolve
to seeking hearts,
stirred to faith.

Across an ocean
there awaited
a land to till,
a harvest to reap,
freedom to worship—
a gathering awaits,
with the Good Book in hand lighting their way,
across the shining sea did sail,
to a shore of hope all disembarked.

They knelt in prayer,
gave thanks to God,
blessed the land and planted the dream
for generations to come.

CAROL ENDRES

AMERICA

3

For where does one run to when he's already in the promised land?

CLAUDE BROWN

The LORD said..."I have come down to rescue them...and to bring them up out of that land into a good and spacious land, a land flowing with milk and honey."

THE BOOK OF EXODUS

America is a promised land, a land of milk and honey. Sheep grazing on hills and clear skies with beckoning stars remind us of God's hand on our land.

CAROL ENDRES

I just want to do God's will. And he's allowed me to go to the mountain. And I've looked over, and I've seen the promised land! I may not get there with you, but I want you to know tonight that we as a people will get to the promised land.

MARTIN LUTHER KING, JR.

Know that the LORD is God. It is he who made us, and we are his; we are his people, the sheep of his pasture.

THE BOOK OF PSALMS

HE DETERMINES THE NUMBER OF THE

STARS AND CALLS THEM EACH BY NAME.

THE BOOK OF PSALMS

The prayer of the farmer kneeling in his field to weed it, the prayer of the rower kneeling with the stroke of his oar, are true prayers heard throughout nature.

RALPH WALDO EMERSON

Through the ample open door of the peaceful country barn,
A sun-lit pasture field, with cattle and horses feeding;
And haze, and vista, and the far horizon, fading away.

WALT WHITMAN
"A Farm-Picture"

AMERICA'S BARNS AND QUILT~LIKE FIELDS BOAST OF A BLESSED LAND.

CAROL ENDRES

Claude was well enough to go into the fields before the harvest was over. The middle of July came, and the farmers were still cutting grain. The yield of wheat and oats was so heavy that there were not machines enough to thrash it within the usual time. Men had to await their turn, letting their grain stand in shock until a belching black engine lumbered into the field. Rains would have been disastrous; but this was one of those "good years" which farmers tell about, when everything goes well. At the time they needed rain, there was plenty of it; and now the days were miracles of dry, glittering heat.

WILLA CATHER

We plow the fields and scatter
The good seed on the land,
But it is fed and watered
By God's almighty hand;
He sends the snow in winter,
The warmth to swell the grain,
The breezes and the sunshine,
And soft refreshing rain.

MATTHIAS CLAUDIUS

AMERICA IS A GATEWAY OF FREEDOM TO

Our flag is red, white and blue, but our nation is a rainbow—red, yellow, brown, black and white—and we're all precious in God's sight.

JESSE JACKSON

YOU'RE A GRAND OLD FLAG;
YOU'RE A HIGH~FLYING FLAG.
AND FOREVER IN PEACE MAY YOU WAVE.

GEORGE COHAN

We hold these truths to be self-evident, that all men are created equal, that they are endowed by their Creator with certain unalienable rights, that among these are life, liberty, and the pursuit of happiness.

THOMAS JEFFERSON

The flag and the Constitution stand for democracy and not tyranny, for freedom, not subjection.

FRANKLIN D. ROOSEVELT

8

LIFE, LIBERTY, AND THE PURSUIT OF HAPPINESS.

CAROL ENDRES

9

If we obey Jesus' command to love one another, we'll always be "the United States."

CAROL ENDRES

I appeal to you, brothers, in the name of our Lord Jesus Christ, that all of you agree with one another so that there may be no divisions among you and that you may be perfectly united in mind and thought.

THE BOOK OF 1 CORINTHIANS

A new command I give you:
Love one another. As I have loved
you, so you must love one another.
By this all men will know
that you are my disciples,
if you love one another.

THE BOOK OF JOHN

Love is life. All,
everything that
I understand,
I understand only
because I love.
Everything is,
everything exists,
only because I love.
Everything is
united by it alone.
Love is God...

LEO TOLSTOY

WE KNOW THAT ALL THINGS WORK

LOVE ONE ANOTHER

TOGETHER FOR GOOD TO THEM THAT LOVE GOD.

THE BOOK OF ROMANS (KJV)

11

PEACE PUTS FORTH HER

WILLIAM SHAKESPEARE

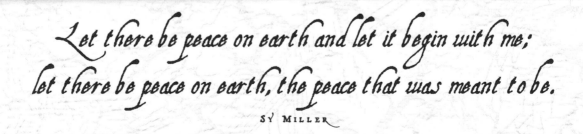

Let there be peace on earth and let it begin with me;
let there be peace on earth, the peace that was meant to be.

SY MILLER

OLIVE EVERYWHERE.

Peace is not the absence of conflict, but the presence of God no matter what the conflict.

AUTHOR UNKNOWN

Blessed are the peacemakers: for they shall be called children of God.

THE BOOK OF MATTHEW

Making peace, I have found, is much harder than making war.

GERRY ADAMS

Let there be peace in our country and let it begin in our homes.

CAROL ENDRES

Creative force, like a musical composer, goes on unweariedly repeating a simple air or theme, now high, now low, in solo, in chorus, ten thousand times reverberated, till it fills earth and heaven with the chant.

RALPH WALDO EMERSON

Creativity has been built into every one of us; it's part of our design. Each of us lives less of the life God intended for us when we choose not to live out the creative powers we possess.

TED ENGSTROM

All things without us, nay I may add, all things on us, are mere elements: but deep within us lies the creative force, which out of these can produce what they were meant to be; and which leaves us neither sleep nor rest, till in one way or another, without us or on us, that same have been produced.

J. W. VON GOETHE

Thou wilt not blame...
The humblest of this band who dares to hope
That unto him hath also been vouchsafed
An insight that in some sort he possesses,
A privilege whereby a work of his,
Proceeding from a source of untaught things,
Creative and enduring, may become
A power like one of Nature's.

WILLIAM WORDSWORTH

EVERYDAY LIFE IN

THE GERANIUM MAN

AMERICA HAS A CREATIVE FORCE BEHIND IT.

CAROL ENDRES

15

APPLES

HOW MANY

ARE IN AN

APPLE SEED

LET THE MOST BEAUTIFUL OR THE SWIFTEST HAVE IT. THAT SHOULD BE THE "GOING" PRICE OF APPLES.

HENRY DAVID THOREAU

It migrates with man, like the dog and horse and cow: first, perchance, from Greece to Italy, thence to England, thence to America; and our Western emigrant is still marching steadily toward the setting sun with the seeds of the apple in his pocket, or perhaps a few young trees strapped to his load....For when man migrates, he carries with him not only his birds, quadrupeds, insects, vegetables, and his very sword, but his orchard also.

HENRY DAVID THOREAU

The first reliable trace of our modest hero finds him in the Territory of Ohio, in 1801, with a horse-load of apple seeds, which he planted in various places on and about the borders of Licking Creek, the first orchard thus originated by him...It was "Johnny Appleseed," by which name Jonathan Chapman was afterward known.

HARPER'S NEW MONTHLY, 1871

A little red apple
Hung high in a tree.
I looked up at it,
And it looked down at me.
"Come down, please," I called.
And what do you suppose?
That little red apple
Dropped right on my nose!

CHILDREN'S POEM

The charm of fishing is that it is the pursuit of what is elusive but attainable, a perpetual series of occasions for hope.

JOHN BUCHAN

Fishing is much more than fish...It is the great occasion when we may return to the fine simplicity of our forefathers.

HERBERT HOOVER

As Jesus was walking beside the Sea of Galilee, he saw two brothers, Simon called Peter and his brother Andrew. They were casting a net into the lake, for they were fishermen. "Come, follow me," Jesus said, "and I will make you fishers of men." At once they left their nets and followed him.

THE BOOK OF MATTHEW

Man can learn a lot from fishing—when the fish are biting no problem in the world is big enough to be remembered.

ORLANDO A. BATTISTA

Early in the morning, while all things are crisp with frost, men come with fishing-reels and slender lunch, and let down their fine lines through the snowy field to take pickerel and perch.

HENRY DAVID THOREAU

THE AMERICAN PASTIME OF FISHING BRINGS

FOOD TO THE TABLE AND PEACE TO THE SOUL.

CAROL ENDRES

Christianity is the root of all democracy,

There is what I call the American idea... This idea demands, as the proximate organization thereof, a democracy,—that is, a government of all the people, by all the people, for all the people. For shortness' sake I will call it the idea of Freedom.

THEODORE PARKER

AMERICAN DEMOCRACY — FOR THE PEOPLE AND BY THE PEOPLE.

America is a land of wonders, in which everything is in constant motion and every change seems an improvement...No natural boundary seems to be set to the efforts of man; and in his eyes, what is not yet done is only what he has not yet attempted to do.

ALEXIS DE TOCQUEVILLE

Democracy is based upon the conviction that there are extraordinary possibilities in ordinary people.

HARRY EMERSON FOSDICK

the highest fact in the rights of men.

NOVALIS

Strength of character may be learned at work,

but beauty of character is learned at home.

HENRY DRUMMOND

The potential possibilities of any child are the most intriguing and stimulating in all creation.

RAY L. WILBUR

TRAIN A CHILD IN THE WAY HE SHOULD GO, AND WHEN HE IS OLD HE WILL NOT TURN FROM IT.

THE BOOK OF PROVERBS

There is the unrestricted and full joy of a child's laughter, uncluttered by the worries of the rest of the world, just affirming the pure unbridled joy of discovering God's world—sharing that joy through their laughter.

GERALD BRIAN THOMAS

May our children come in and eat at the table of kind and sweet words, and may they go out and speak the same to the world.

CAROL ENDRES

CHILDREN ARE POOR MEN'S RICHES.

ENGLISH PROVERB

We can't form our children on our own concepts; we must take them and love them as God gives them to us.

J. W. VON GOETHE

Section 1 = Getting to know
someone, such as God or people out
in the world. (To know what to do,
when problems hit.)
Section 2 = He's the leader!!
and some bible passages.
Section 3 = The 5 yr. memory(ies)

I have a Constitution hardy enough to encounter and undergo the most severe trials, and, I flatter myself, resolution to face what any Man durst, as shall be prov'd when it comes to the Test.

GEORGE WASHINGTON

24

AMERICA

True bravery means doing alone that which one could do if all the world were by.

FRANÇOIS, DUC DE LA ROCHEFOUCAULD

DON'T BE AFRAID. HAVE NOT I GIVEN YOU THIS ORDER? BE STRONG AND BRAVE.

THE BOOK OF 2 SAMUEL

AND THIS BE OUR MOTTO—IN GOD IS OUR TRUST
AND THE STAR SPANGLED BANNER IN TRIUMPH
SHALL WAVE, O'ER THE LAND OF THE
FREE, AND THE HOME OF THE BRAVE!

"HOME OF THE BRAVE"

It is wonderful what
strength of purpose
and boldness and
energy of will
are roused by the
assurance that we
are doing our duty.

WALTER SCOTT

*Bravery is the capacity to perform
properly even when scared half to death.*

OMAR BRADLEY

25

HOME OF THE BRAVE

Gold is good in its place, but living, brave,

OUR SOLDIERS PAY THE PRICE FOR AMERICA'S FREEDOM.

CAROL ENDRES

These are the times that try men's souls. The summer soldier and the sunshine patriot will, in this crisis, shrink from the service of their country; but he that stands it now, deserves the love and thanks of man and woman.

THOMAS PAINE

The history of the world is full of men who rose to leadership, by sheer force of self-confidence, bravery and tenacity.

MAHATMA GANDHI

We have enjoyed so much freedom for so long that we are perhaps in danger of forgetting how much blood it cost to establish the Bill of Rights.

FELIX FRANKFURTER

patriotic men are better than gold.

ABRAHAM LINCOLN

27

Be grateful for the home you have, knowing

Round the hearthstone of home,
In the land of our birth,
The holiest spot on the face
of the earth.

GEORGE POPE MORRIS

LOOK WELL TO THE HEARTHSTONE;
THEREIN ALL HOPE FOR AMERICA LIVES.

CALVIN COOLIDGE

Give me your tired, your poor,
Your huddled masses yearning to breathe free,
The wretched refuse of your teeming shore.
Send these, the homeless, tempest-tossed to me,
I lift my lamp beside the golden door!

EMMA LAZARUS

A person can run for years
but sooner or later he has to
take a stand in the place
which, for better or worse,
he calls home, doing what he
can to change things there.

PAULE MARSHALL

HOME IS WHERE THE HEART OF AMERICA IS.

CAROL ENDRES

that at this moment, all you have is all you need.

SARAH BAN BREATHNACH

LAND OF THE FREE

QUEEN BEE ANGEL

We make a living by what we get, but we

A strong nation, like a strong person, can afford to be gentle, firm, thoughtful, and restrained. It can afford to extend a helping hand to others.

JIMMY CARTER

KINDNESS IS ALWAYS FASHIONABLE.

AMELIA E. BARR

Human kindness has never weakened the stamina or softened the fiber of a free people. A nation does not have to be cruel in order to be tough.

FRANKLIN D. ROOSEVELT

America is the Queen of bee-ing giving and thoughtful to all.

CAROL ENDRES

make a life by what we give.

NORMAN MACEWAN

31

GOD BLESSED AMERICA BECAUSE IT WAS

I consider it an indispensable duty to close this last solemn act of my Official life, by commending the Interest of our dearest Country to the protection of Almighty God, and those who have the superintendence of them, to his holy keeping.

GEORGE WASHINGTON

Let our object be our country, our whole country, and nothing but our country. And, by the blessing of God, may that country itself become a vast and splendid monument, not of oppression and terror, but of wisdom, of peace, and of liberty, upon which the world may gaze with admiration forever.

DANIEL WEBSTER

Thy love divine hath led us in the past,
In this free land by Thee our lot is cast;
Be Thou our ruler, guardian, guide, and stay,
Thy Word our law, Thy paths our chosen way.

DANIEL ROBERTS

"Light"

Alexa Weinhold
M:
Katrina

FOUNDED ON CHRIST AND HIS PRINCIPLES.

CAROL ENDRES

In this way we are reaffirming the transcendence of religious faith in America's heritage and future; in this way we shall constantly strengthen those spiritual weapons which forever will be our country's most powerful resource in peace and war.

DWIGHT D. EISENHOWER

Our pilgrim fathers

WE WILL EITHER BE GOVERNED

knew what they were looking for—Freedom.

CAROL ENDRES

Having undertaken for the Glory of
God, and Advancement
of the Christian
Faith, and the
Honour of our
King and Country, a Voyage
to plant the first Colony in
the northern Parts of Virginia;
Do by these Presents,
solemnly and mutually, in
the Presence of God and one another,
covenant and combine ourselves together
into a civil Body Politick, for our better
Ordering and Preservation.

THE MAYFLOWER COMPACT

My country, 'tis of thee,
Sweet land of liberty, Of thee I sing:
Land where my fathers died,
Land of the pilgrims' pride,
From every mountain side
Let freedom ring!

SAMUEL F. SMITH

Ah! Freedom is a noble thing!
Freedom makes man to have liking:
Freedom all solace to man gives:
He lives at ease that freely lives!

JOHN BARBOUR

BY GOD OR RULED BY TYRANTS.

WILLIAM PENN

35

AMERICA HAS SET A PATTERN OF THE PEOPLE, BY THE PEOPLE, FOR THE PEOPLE,

CAROL ENDRES

Once I prophesied that this generation of Americans had a rendezvous with destiny. That prophecy comes true. To us much is given, more is expected. This generation will "nobly save or meanly lose the last best hope of earth...The way is plain, peaceful, generous, just—a way, which if followed, the world will forever applaud, and God must forever bless."

FRANKLIN D. ROOSEVELT

Therefore let us choose life that we, and our seed may live; by obeying His voice, and clinging to Him, for He is our life, and our prosperity.

JOHN WINTHROP

36

FOR ALL ITS GENERATIONS...

Generations come and generations go, but the earth remains forever.

THE BOOK OF ECCLESIASTES

Liberty, the precious boon of Heaven, is meek and reasonable. She admits that she belongs to all—to the high and the low, the rich and the poor, the black and the white—and that she belongs to them all equally.

GERRIT SMITH

37

R OWN FRUIT · PICK YOUR OWN FRUIT · PICK YOUR

LIGHT UP YOUR WORLD WITH LOVE

Love brings freedom—that's what

38

Love...keeps no record of wrongs.

THE BOOK OF 1 CORINTHIANS

PERFECT LOVE CASTS OUT FEAR.

THE BOOK OF 1 JOHN

Faith, like light,
should always be
simple and unbending;
while love, like warmth,
should beam forth
on every side and
bend to every necessity
of our brethren.

MARTIN LUTHER

Mortals, while through the world you go,
Hope may succor and faith befriend,
Yet happy your hearts if you can but know,
Love awaits at the journey's end.

CLINTON SCOLLARD

LOVE MAKES ONE FIT FOR ANY WORK.

AUTHOR UNKNOWN

you'll find going on in this land.

CAROL ENDRES

39

Patriotism is not short, frenzied outbursts of emotion, but the tranquil and steady dedication of a lifetime.

ADLAI STEVENSON

Behold, how good and how pleasant it is for brethren to dwell together in unity!

THE BOOK OF PSALMS (KJV)

⭐ ⭐ ⭐ ⭐ ⭐ ⭐ ⭐ ⭐ ⭐ ⭐ ⭐

The spirit of truth and the spirit of freedom—they are the pillars of society.

HENRIK IBSEN

In necessary things, unity; in disputed things, liberty; in all things, charity.

RICHARD BAXTER

SHOUT IT FROM THE TREETOPS: "UNITED WE STAND!"

CAROL ENDRES

Let us put an end to self-inflicted wounds. Let us remember that our national unity is a most priceless asset.

GERALD FORD

THERE'S NO PLACE LIKE HOMETOWN AMERICA. HURRAH, AMERICA!

CAROL ENDRES

America! the land we love!
God's second gift from Heaven above,
Builded and fashioned out of truth
Sinewed by Him with splendid youth
For that glad day when shall be furled
All tyrant flags throughout the world.
For this our banner holds the sky:
That liberty shall never die.
For this, America began:
To make a brotherhood of man.

EDGAR GUEST

Mid pleasures and palaces though we may roam,
Be it ever so humble, there's no place like home;
A charm from the skies seems to hallow us there,
Which, seek through the world, is ne'er met with elsewhere.

Home, home, sweet, sweet home!
There's no place like home!
There's no place like home!

J.H. PAYNE

Nobody knows anything about America

who does not know its little towns.

The Word of God Tends to Make

A glory gilds the sacred page,
Majestic like the sun;
It gives a light to every age,—
It gives but borrows none.

The hand that gave it still supplies
The gracious light and heat;
His truths upon the nations rise,—
They rise but never set.

WILLIAM COWPER

It is each generation's responsibility to pass on to the next generation the Word of God, which this nation was founded upon.

CAROL ENDRES

So great is my veneration for the Bible that the earlier my children begin to read it, the more confident will be my hope that they will prove useful citizens to their country, and respectable members of society.

JOHN QUINCY ADAMS

Hold fast to the Bible as the sheet-anchor of your liberties; write its precepts in your hearts, and practice them in your lives. To the influence of this book we are indebted for all the progress made in true civilization, and to this we must look as our guide in the future. "Righteousness exalteth a nation; but sin is a reproach to any people."

ULYSSES S. GRANT

LARGE~MINDED, NOBLE~HEARTED MEN.

HENRY WARD BEECHER

I have been driven many times to my knees by the

Celebrate freedom every day by praising God for it and praying for America's leaders.

CAROL ENDRES

We commend this nation to thy merciful care, that being guided by thy Providence, we may dwell secure in thy peace. Grant to the president of the United States, and to all in authority, wisdom and strength to know and to do thy will. Fill them with the love of truth and righteousness; and make them ever mindful of their calling to serve this people in thy fear.

THE BOOK OF COMMON PRAYER

Freedom—no word was ever spoken that has held out greater hope, demanded greater sacrifice, needed more to be nurtured, blessed more the giver...or came closer to being God's will on earth.

OMAR N. BRADLEY

EXAMPLE IS LEADERSHIP.

ALBERT SCHWEITZER

There is only one true liberty—the liberty of Jesus at work in our conscience enabling us to do what is right.

OSWALD CHAMBERS

Long may our land be bright
With Freedom's holy light;
Protect us by Thy might,
Great God, our King.

SAMUEL FRANCIS SMITH

overwhelming conviction that I had nowhere else to go.

ABRAHAM LINCOLN

47

I PLEDGE ALLEGIANCE TO THE FLAG OF THE UNITED STATES OF AMERICA AND TO THE REPUBLIC FOR WHICH IT STANDS ONE NATION UNDER GOD INDIVISIBLE WITH LIBERTY AND JUSTICE FOR ALL.

CAROL ENDRIS

O BEAUTIFUL FOR SPACIOUS SKIES,
FOR AMBER WAVES OF GRAIN,
FOR PURPLE MOUNTAIN MAJESTIES
ABOVE THE FRUITED PLAIN!
AMERICA! AMERICA!
GOD SHED HIS GRACE ON THEE,
AND CROWN THY GOOD WITH BROTHERHOOD
FROM SEA TO SHINING SEA.

KATHARINE LEE BATES